HEINEMANN
Profiles

Anne Frank

An Unauthorized Biography

Richard Tames

Heinemann Library
Des Plaines, Illinois

Designed by Visual Image
Printed in Hong Kong / China

03 02 01 00 99

10 9 8 7 6 5 4 3 2 1

Library of Congress Cataloging-in-Publication Data
Tames, Richard.
  Anne Frank / Richard Tames.
    p.   cm. — (Heinemann profiles)
  Includes bibliographical references and index.
  Summary: Traces the life of a Jewish girl who chronicled her day
-to-day life in a diary as she hid in an attic in Nazi-occupied
Holland for two years.
  ISBN 1-57572-690-4 (lib. bdg.)
    1. Frank, Anne 1929-1945—Juvenile literature. 2. Holocaust,
Jewish (1939-1945)—Netherlands—Amsterdam—Biography—Juvenile
literature. 3. Jews—Netherlands—Amsterdam—Biography—Juvenile
literature. 4. Jewish children in the Holocaust—Biography
—Juvenile literature. 5. Amsterdam (Netherlands)—Biography
—Juvenile literature. [1. Frank, Anne, 1929-1945. 2. Jews
—Netherlands—Biography. 3. Holocaust, Jewish (1939-1945)
—Netherlands—Amsterdam. 4. Women—Biography.] I. Title.
II. Series.
DS135.N6F736   1998
940.53'18'092—dc21
  [b]   98-23295
                                                       CIP
                                                        AC

Acknowledgments
The publisher would like to thank the following for permission to reproduce photographs: AKG Photo, pp. 4, 5; 8, 14, 39; Anne Frank Stichting, pp. 6, 15, 23, 26 (e, f, g), 32, 38; Benelux Press b.v., pp. 25, 26 (a, b, d, h), 28, 30; Chris Honeywell, p. 49; Historisches Museum, Frankfurt-am-Main, p. 11; Miep Gies, p. 17; Popperfoto, pp. 26 (c), 44; Rijksintituut voor Oologsdocumentatie, pp. 18, 19, 37, 41; Spaarnestad Fotoarchief, pp. 10, 16, 20, 27, 31, 35, 36, 40, 42, 45; Topsham Picturepoint, pp.7, 47.

Cover photograph reproduced with permission of Wiener Library

Every effort has been made to contact copyright holders of any material reproduced in this book. Any omissions will be rectified in subsequent printings if notice is given to the Publisher.

Any words appearing in the text in bold, **like this,** are explained in the Glossary.

This book includes extracts from Anne Frank, *The Diary of a Young Girl The Definitive Edition*, edited by Otto H. Frank and Mirjam Pressler, translated by Susan Massotty, Penguin Books 1997.

This is an unauthorized biography. The subject has not sponsored or endorsed this book.

CONTENTS

WHO WAS ANNE FRANK?

In 1933 the **Nazis** came to power in Germany. They began to **persecute** everyone they considered enemies or opponents. Highest on their list were Jews. By 1945, when World War II ended, at least six million Jews—possibly more—would be dead, shot, gassed, beaten, or worked to death. Others died of cold, hunger, or disease. Anne Frank, herself born in Germany, was one of those millions. But unlike most of those whose lives were so brutally cut short, her words still reach out from beyond her grave, wherever that may be.

Anne Frank in 1942, the year she and her family went into hiding.

THE TEENAGER

Almost as soon as Anne Frank became a teenager, she had to give up her friends, her pleasures, and even her pet cat to go into hiding from the Nazis. When she might have been going out dating and dancing, she spent years in hiding, wishing the days away. She could see a world outside but never take part in it because for her it meant danger and death. She recorded her dreams and fears in the diary she called "Kitty." Kitty became the best friend that she felt she had never had.

THE WRITER

Writing to Kitty passed long days but also helped Anne to examine her feelings and understand herself better. She decided that when she grew up, she would earn her living as a writer.

Pages from Anne's diary; the picture in the diary is of Anne herself. Unlike other writers, Anne Frank could only travel from one floor to another, and saw no one but the same dozen people, day in, day out, from one year's end to the next. She lived like a prisoner, but she fought to keep her mind free.

EPITAPH

Anne Frank's short life ended in squalor and misery, separated from all who had loved her. Anne dreamed that one day she would grow up to become a famous writer. She did become a famous writer, but she never had the chance to grow up to be an adult.

Where Anne Frank lived and died

Amsterdam
Westerbork ★④
③ Osnabrück ⑥ ★ Bergen-Belsen POLAND
THE NETHERLANDS Berlin
BELGIUM ②Aachen GERMANY Auschwitz-Birkenau
①Frankfurt am Main ★⑤
FRANCE

★ Concentration camp
.... Railway line
①-⑥ Places where Anne Frank lived

THE FRANK FAMILY

The Frank family first settled in the German city of Frankfurt-am-Main in the seventeenth century. Frankfurt grew rich on trade and finance, and as the city prospered, so did the Frank family. Anne Frank's grandfather was a banker. Her father, Otto, briefly studied art at a university. At the age of 20, he decided to join a friend in America and work in Macy's, the famous New York department store. A year later, Otto's father died. Otto went back to Germany and got a job in an engineering factory in the industrial city of Dusseldorf.

World War I broke out when Otto was 25. Both he and two of his brothers served in the army. Otto rose to the rank of lieutenant. After the war he went to work with the bank that his father had worked for.

MARRIAGE AND A FAMILY

In 1925 Otto Frank married Edith Hollander, who came from Aachen in northern Germany, near the border with the Netherlands. Otto was by now quite well-to-do, so they had a honeymoon in Italy. Then they settled in Frankfurt.

Anne Frank's father, Otto, *(right)* served in the German army during World War I.

Otto Frank with his two daughters, Margot *(left)* and baby Anne

For the first two years, they lived with Otto's mother before moving into a home of their own. Their first child, Margot Betti, was born in 1926. In 1929 they had a second daughter. They called her Annelies Marie, Anne for short. Taking care of two small children kept Edith very busy, but Otto was able to pay for a housemaid, Kathi, to help her. Otto was also an avid amateur photographer and took many pictures of his growing family.

THE GREAT DEPRESSION

For people in business, 1929 was a terrible year. The prosperity of the United States, the richest country in the world, suddenly collapsed. Many banks lost huge sums that they had loaned to businesses, so they were unable to pay people who had trusted them with their savings. Every country that did business with the United States was affected. Throughout Europe people rushed to take their savings out of banks. Factories closed down. Millions of people lost their jobs.

Unemployed people line up in Germany. Notice the Hitler slogan and swastika on the wall of the building.

By 1932 the factories in Frankfurt were only making a third of the goods they had manufactured in 1929, and 70,000 of the city's residents were unemployed. One person in four had no regular income. Soup kitchens were opened to give a basic meal to people living in poverty. People were frightened and angry, and they found it difficult to understand why things were going wrong.

Moving on

Otto Frank was lucky. He still had a job. He also had a happy family and a pleasant home in the suburbs. But in 1933 he decided to give up everything he had worked for and take his family to start all over again in a foreign country, the Netherlands. This was because 1933 was the year in which Adolf Hitler and the **Nazi** Party came to power in Germany. Hitler and the Nazis blamed Germany's problems on the Jews, many of whom were important in banking and other types of business.

Frankfurt had a Jewish population of 30,000, who accounted for just over one-twentieth of the city's population. Throughout Germany only Berlin had a larger Jewish community. The Frank family were part of Frankfurt's Jewish community. With the Nazis in power, Otto swiftly decided that Germany, the country he had fought for in World War I, was no longer safe for him and his family.

THE RISE OF THE NAZIS

Germany was defeated in World War I. Although no enemy set foot on German land, its people were near starving, so the government gave up fighting. Many ordinary German soldiers believed they had been betrayed, not beaten, and were furious. One of those soldiers was Adolf Hitler.

HITLER, ARYANS AND JEWS

Hitler was not born in Germany but in Austria. As a young man, he dreamed of becoming a great artist, but he was lazy and ended up living little better than a bum. Hitler began to develop ideas about why the world had failed to make him a success.

Nazis parade up and down the streets with notices saying "Germans! Beware! Don't buy from Jews."

He believed that people could be divided into different races and that conflict between races was the key to history. Hitler declared that the most superior people were the Aryans of northern Europe, who ought to be united as a single nation and rule the whole world. Other races, such as the Slavs of eastern Europe (Russians, Poles, and others), Asians, Africans, and especially Jews, ought to work as slaves for the Aryans until they died out altogether.

As Nazis take over the local town hall in Frankfurt, a German crowd gives the Nazi salute. Notice the Nazi swastika flag on the balcony.

THE NAZIS EMERGE

During World War I, Hitler joined the German army, won two medals for bravery, and enjoyed army life. Hitler blamed the Jews for Germany's defeat. He said they only wanted to make money and cared nothing for Germany. This completely ignored the fact that many Jews, like Otto Frank and his brothers, had served bravely in the army during the war.

In 1919 Hitler joined a small new political group, the National Socialist German Workers' Party, Nazis for short. He soon became its leader, promising to make Germany the greatest country in the world. The Nazis had their own private army, the **SA** (*Sturmabteilungen*, or Stormtroopers), to beat up their opponents, especially **communists**. The parades and uniforms appealed to many unemployed ex-soldiers.

The morning after "Kristallnacht," The windows of a Jewish-owned shop have been smashed by a Nazi mob.

THE NAZIS IN POWER

When the Great Depression of 1929 threw the country into crisis, more and more people began to listen to Hitler. He promised to lead Germany to a bright future. In 1933 Hitler finally became head of the government. Within months he began to make himself a **dictator** and started to **persecute** Germany's Jews.

On April 1, 1933, Germans were told by the new Nazi government that they should not buy goods in shops owned by Jews or use the services of Jewish doctors and lawyers. Jews were not allowed to be teachers either. By the end of 1933, 150,000 people opposed to the Nazis had been arrested and sent to **concentration camps**. In 1935 marriage between **Aryans** and Jews was made illegal.

Between November 9 and 11, 1938, dozens of **synagogues** and thousands of Jewish shops were smashed up and set on fire by mobs. The police did nothing. This nationwide riot was known as 'Kristallnacht' (the night of breaking glass). The following day, 30,000 Jewish men and boys were arrested and sent to concentration camps. Many Jews realized that things were only going to get worse and that they had to escape. By the spring of 1939, half of Germany's 500,000 Jews had left the country. Meanwhile Hitler continued to prepare for a war to put all of Europe under German leadership.

A New Home in a New Country

Otto Frank chose to take his family to the Netherlands because it had a long history of welcoming foreigners. Amsterdam, the biggest city, had a large Jewish community. During World War I, the Netherlands had been **neutral**, taking no part in the fighting. A peaceful, prosperous, neighboring country seemed like a safe place for the family. Of course, they would have to speak Dutch, but the children were young and would learn easily.

Moving in stages

In 1933 Mrs. Frank took Margot and Anne with her to Aachen, near the Dutch border, to live with her mother, while Mr. Frank went ahead to Amsterdam. He had to find a new home and start up a new business. The business was a branch of a German company called Opekta, which made pectin, a substance used to make jams and jellies gel, or set

The Frank family on the way to the wedding of Otto's secretary, Miep Gies

Anne (arrowed) in class at her new Dutch school

solid. Edith and Margot joined him in December 1933. Anne joined them in February 1934, as soon as their new home was fully furnished.

GETTING ALONG WELL

The Frank family home was in a bright, new suburb. It was a third-floor apartment, looking out onto a park. It had a flat roof in the back for sunbathing in warm weather. As more new homes were built nearby, other families moved in, and the children soon had many friends: Jewish, Catholic, and Protestant. There was little car traffic, so it was safe to play in the streets. Margot and Anne could go shopping or to the movies downtown with their mother, and the seaside was not far away.

The Franks had
a new home
in a new
neighborhood.
They lived in a
large block of
housing looking
out onto a park,
newly planted
with trees and
shrubs.

Of course, the girls also had to go to school. They were soon both getting very good report cards, but Anne was quite a chatterbox and often had to do extra homework as a punishment for talking when she should have been paying attention.

Anne was often angry with her older sister because Margot was praised by her parents for being quiet and tidy and taking good care of her clothes. Anne's favorite interests were pets, movie stars, Greek myths, riding her bicycle, and going to a local ice-cream parlor called Oasis.

Mr. Frank's business did so well that he had to hire new staff. One of them, Miep Santrouschitz, was an Austrian who became a close family friend. Later she married a Dutchman, Henk Gies, and became Mrs. Miep Gies.

In 1938 Mr. Frank started a second company to sell herbs for seasoning meat. His partner in the new venture was Mr. van Daan, another Jewish businessman, who had also left his home in Germany, bringing his wife and son, Peter, with him.

DANGER AHEAD?

Mr. Frank continued to worry about the news from Germany, where conditions became worse and worse for Jews. In 1938 Mrs. Frank's two brothers managed to escape to the United States. Her mother came to live in the Netherlands.

Otto Frank posed with his secretary Miep, who would later bring the Frank family their food when they were in hiding.

Britain, France, and Germany seemed almost ready to go to war with each other that year, but the crisis passed. In 1939 Britain and France finally did go to war with Germany when it invaded Poland. But the Netherlands was expected to remain **neutral** again and stay out of the fighting.

Conquered!

Invasion

On May 10, 1940, Germany invaded the Netherlands without warning, taking the Dutch armed forces completely by surprise. The Dutch royal family and government fled to Britain. German bombers raided the port of Rotterdam, destroying over 24,000 houses and killing almost 1,000 people. By May 15, the Netherlands was under German control.

New rulers, new rules

Dutch people soon found that everyone had to carry an identity card and that their food was rationed.

German paratroops invade the Netherlands. The speed and power of the German forces ended the fighting in a matter of days.

BOSBAD

Herinnering Nederland 10 Mei 19

Life was to be far worse for the 140,000 Jews in the Netherlands. In October 1940, all Jewish businesses were required to register with the German authorities. Mr. Frank realized that this meant that the Germans were planning to take them over. So he transferred his business into the name of trusted Dutch friends.

All Jews, adults and children, were forced to wear a yellow star with the word "Jew" on it. In June 1941, all Jews had the letter "J" stamped on their identity card so that they could be picked out more easily. In September 1941, Margot and Anne were forced to leave their school and go to a separate school where there were only Jewish pupils and teachers.

German troops arrest people suspected of wanting to fight back. Most would be imprisoned and many shot. Often their families never knew what had happened to them.

A PEOPLE APART

From May 1942 on, all Jews over the age of six had to wear on their clothes a yellow Star of David badge with the word "Jew" on it. This meant that any Jew could be instantly identified on sight. Many people feared that even being seen talking to a Jewish friend or neighbor would mean trouble.

Jews were banned from trains and forbidden to own cars or even bicycles. All their shopping had to be done between 3:00 and 5:00 in the afternoon and only in special Jewish shops. Jews had to stay indoors from 8:00 each evening until 6:00 the next morning. They had to get their hair cut only at Jewish barbershops. They were banned from using public swimming pools.

At first Anne found the hiding place exciting: "like being on holiday in a very strange **pension**." (July 11, 1942, p. 26) But a holiday is a time for going out, playing, and having fun. Anne had to learn to sit still for hours at a time. No noisy chattering now because it might be heard outside.

The Franks were a loving and happy family, but cooped up together, they soon began to find daily life difficult. Mr. and Mrs. Frank hated the nearby church clock, which chimed every fifteen minutes, day and night. At night Margot's coughing woke Anne up. A week after the Franks moved into the secret annex they were joined by Mr. and Mrs. van Daan and their teenage son, Peter. So everyone was even more confined. And Mrs. van Daan soon made it clear that she thought Anne was a nuisance.

Anne and Margot shared a room. They put up pictures and postcards to brighten up the walls.

THE DAILY ROUTINE

In November 1942, the seven people in the annex were joined by an eighth, Mr. Dussel. Mr. Frank thought there was no more risk in hiding eight than seven, and it would mean one more safe from the **Nazis**. Besides, Mr. Dussel was a dentist, which might be very useful, since no one with a toothache could go out for treatment.

With eight people living in six rooms, daily life had to be carefully organized.

In hiding: the eight people confined together in the annex were a) Mr. Frank, b) Mrs. Frank , c) Anne, d) Margot, e) Mr. van Daan, f) Mr. Dussel, g) Mrs. van Daan, h) Peter van Daan

Otto Frank's office building was at 263 Prinsengracht. The door on the far left led up to the annex; the middle door led to the second floor office; and the door on the right led to the ground floor warehouse.

Morning

The alarm clock rang at 6:45 A.M. each morning. Everyone took turns using the bathroom. The boys who worked downstairs in the warehouse arrived by 8:30 A.M. They knew nothing about the hiding place, so everybody in the annex had to have finished washing by then, since sounds of running water would make the workers suspicious.

A breakfast of bread and coffee was eaten at 9:00 A.M. in the van Daans' room, on the top floor, where any noise was least likely to be heard. For the same reason, it was essential for everyone to sit as still as possible for the rest of the morning. Slippers, not shoes, were worn by anyone needing to move.

This picture shows Anne and her books, before she was confined to the annex. Mr. Frank made sure that Anne, Margot, and Peter tried to keep up with the schoolwork they were missing. Anne liked learning, especially history, but hated mathematics.

AFTERNOON

The warehouse boys went for lunch at 12:30 P.M., so the hiders could move around freely until they came back at 2:00 P.M. During the lunch break the helpers from the office below would come up to have a bowl of soup and listen to BBC news. The rest of the working day was spent sleeping, reading, writing, or helping with office paperwork. Anne learned to write in shorthand.

EVENING

After the office and warehouse closed, it was possible to move around again. Anne got some exercise by practicing ballet steps. The evening meal, consisting mainly of vegetables, was prepared and eaten. Housework and washing could be done without worrying about the noise of running water or furniture being moved. After listening to the BBC again, it would be time to take turns in the bathroom and get ready for bed. As the youngest, Anne went first.

Burglars

Just over a year after the Franks moved into the secret annex, the Prinsengracht building was robbed. One Thursday night, thieves forced their way in with a crowbar. Anne noted their haul in her diary: "… two cash boxes containing 40 guilders, blank checkbooks, and worst of all, **[ration] coupons** for 320 pounds of sugar." (July 16, 1943, p. 114)

Another burglary occurred in March 1944. Once again the hiders wondered whether the intruders had heard them or noticed anything suspicious. But nothing came of it.

A third break-in took place on Sunday, April 9, 1944. This was much more frightening. The four men went downstairs. Mr. van Daan tried a bold bluff and shouted, "Police!" The burglars ran off and the men came back upstairs. But because the street door had been broken down a neighbor sent for the police. Naturally they searched the building:

… a noise below… Footsteps in the house, the private office, the kitchen, then… on the staircase. All sounds of breathing stopped, eight hearts pounded… then a rattling at the bookcase… then we heard a [can] fall, and the footsteps receded… I heard several sets of teeth chattering, no one said a word.   (April 11, 1944, p. 253)

THE WAR GOES ON

When Mr. Dussel joined the hiders in November 1942, he brought them up-to-date on what had been happening to other Dutch Jews. Anne recorded in her diary with horror,

… night after night, green and grey military vehicles cruise the streets. They knock on every door, asking whether any Jews live there. If so, the whole family is immediately taken away… It's impossible to escape their clutches unless you go into hiding… No one is spared… all are marched to their death.

(November 19, 1942, p. 72-3)

TURNING THE TIDE

From the outbreak of war in 1939, right up to the time the Franks went into hiding in July 1942, the armies of **Nazi** Germany seemed unbeatable. But from 1943 on, the fighting began to go against them. Every night British and American bombers flew over Amsterdam on their way to targets in Germany. Anne was terrified by the antiaircraft fire aimed at them.

I crawl into Father's bed nearly every night for comfort.. I know it sounds childish, but wait till it happens to you! The ack-ack guns make so much noise, you can't hear your own voice.

(March 10, 1943, p. 89)

Destroyed! A registration office, where records about people were kept, is blown up by the Dutch resistance. Without accurate information about individuals, such as their age, appearance, address, and workplace, it would be impossible to know who was on the run or in hiding.

In July 1943, Anne wrote in her diary that the British had landed in Sicily. Mr. Frank hoped that this would be a turning point. The surrender of Italy, Germany's ally, in September 1943 made him hope that the war might even end that year.

On Christmas Eve that year, Anne confided to her diary her feelings of frustration:

> … if you have been shut up for a year and a half, it can get too much for you sometimes… . I long to ride a bike, dance, whistle, look at the world, feel young, and know that I'm free, and yet I can't let it show.
>
> (December 24, 1943, p. 153)

The food in the annex was very plain. Each person's share was measured carefully.

A SETBACK ON THE KITCHEN FRONT

On March 14, 1944, Anne recorded in her diary that the **resistance** workers who supplied them with forged **ration coupons** had been caught. The hiders would have to make do with an even more boring diet than they had already been living on.

… lunch today consists of mashed potatoes and pickled **kale**… you wouldn't believe how much kale can stink when it's a few years old! The kitchen smells like a mixture of spoiled plums, rotten eggs, and **brine**. Ugh, just the thought of having to eat that muck makes me want to be sick!

(March 14, 1944, p. 214)

Since the people in hiding did not officially exist, they had to rely on their helpers to buy forged coupons for food rations.

INVASION!

On June 6, 1944, Anne recorded landings in northern France by **Allied** forces: American, British, Canadian, and soldiers who had escaped from conquered countries, such as France and Poland.

The Allied troops met stiff resistance from the German armies occupying France, but by September 1944, British troops had driven them out of the south of the Netherlands. For the hiders in the annex, however, liberation came too late.

Will this year, 1944, bring us victory? We don't know yet. But where there's hope, there's life. It fills us with fresh courage and makes us strong again… It's now a matter of remaining calm and steadfast, of gritting our teeth and keeping a stiff upper lip!… Oh, Kitty, the best part about the invasion is that I have the feeling that friends are on the way.

(June 6, 1944, p. 309)

ARREST

The last entry in Anne's diary is dated Tuesday August 1, 1944, over two years after the Franks had gone into hiding. On the morning of Friday August 4, Otto Frank went to Peter's room as usual to give him an English lesson. Just as they were about to start, they heard angry voices downstairs. A few minutes later they could hear a scraping noise as the bookcase disguising the entrance to the secret annex was pulled back.

Five men with guns, one a German police officer, burst in. The German, Karl Silberbauer, shouted for them to hand over any valuables they had. Grabbing a briefcase, he threw its contents—including Anne's diary—onto the floor and used it to carry away money and jewelry belonging to the people in the annex. All eight of them were arrested and hustled away to German police headquarters.

The last journey; a list of passengers on the last train from Westerbork to Auschwitz contains the names of the Frank family. Mr. Frank is listed as a trader, the others as having no occupation.

5   5 September   4   Blatt

JUDENTRANSPORT AUS DEN NIEDERLANDEN - LAGER WESTERBORK

Haeftlinge

301. ✓Engers	Isidor — ✓30.4. 93 –	Kaufmann
302 ✓ Engers	Leonard 15.6. 20 –	Lamdarbeiter
303 ✓ Franco	Manfred – ✓1.5. 05 –	Verleger
304. Frank	Arthur 22.8. 81	Kaufmann
305. Frank ×	Isaac ✓29.11.87	Installateur
306. Frank	Margot 16.2. 26	ohne
307. Frank ✓	Otto ✓12.5. 89	Kaufmann
308. ✓ Frank-Hollaender	Edith 16.1. 00	ohne
309. Frank	Anneliese 12.6. 29	ohne
310. v.Franck	Sara – 27.4. 02 –	Typistin
311. Franken	Rozanna 16.5. 96 –	Landarbeiter
312. ✓ Franken-Weyand	Johanna 24.12.96 ✓	Landbauer
313. Franken	Hermann – ✓12.5.34	ohne
314. Franken	Louis 10.8. 17 –	Gaertner

Waiting to go:
Jews gathered
in Amsterdam
to leave for
Westerbork
**concentration
camp.**

BETRAYED

By the autumn of 1944, out of a population of nine million some 300,000 Dutch people had been forced to go to work in Germany. Another 250,000 had gone into hiding to avoid this fate. Almost 20,000 were being held in camps as prisoners of war or because of their political beliefs.

About 25,000 Dutch Jews had gone into hiding. For some, like the people in the annex, this meant living in attics or back rooms or even under the floorboards of a house or barn. In the countryside, however, small children could often be passed off as relatives sent out from the cities to keep them safe from bombing. Of the Dutch Jews who hid, 16,000 survived the war, but 9,000 were either discovered by chance raids or betrayed by **informers**.

Roundup:
German troops
on patrol found
and arrested
Jews in hiding.

People betrayed the Jews for money or because they were Dutch **Nazis** who supported German **persecution** of Jews. The usual payment to an **informer** amounted to about one week's average wages. But sometimes betrayal was caused by threats of arrest or torture. Who betrayed the secret of 263 Prinsengracht, or why, has never been definitely established. A house overlooking the back of the hide-out was occupied by Dutch Nazis who may have noticed lights or movement in the rooms that were supposed to be empty.

SEPARATED

The eight people in the annex were allowed to pack a few clothes. Their two helpers, Mr. Koophuis and Mr. Kraler, were also arrested and sent to a separate prison camp. Both survived. On the day of the arrests, after work was over, Miep, her husband Jan, and other members of the staff went up to the annex and rescued Anne's diary, the Frank family photo album, and other books and papers.

At Westerbork, the Dutch concentration camp, Jews were crowded into flimsy wooden huts.

A week later the secret annex was emptied of everything else on German orders.

Four days after their arrest, the people from the annex were sent to Westerbork for the rest of August. On September 3, they were loaded onto the last train out of the camp and crammed into a boxcar with 70 others, headed for Auschwitz **concentration camp** in Poland. When they got there two days later, the men and the women were separated from each other. The old, sick, and those under fifteen and were judged too weak even for slave labor were sent to be executed in the gas chambers the very next day. Anne was just fifteen, so she was sent to the nearby women's camp at Birkenau, along with her sister and mother and Mrs. van Daan. It was the last time she saw her adored father.

Starvation and Liberation

Strike!

In September 1944, the Dutch government in London ordered Dutch railway workers to strike so that German forces could not move supplies around the Netherlands. The **resistance** groups added to the chaos by blowing up railway lines. The Germans hit back by taking livestock, food supplies, machinery, and even bicycles to Germany. They also stopped the movement of all food and fuel from the countryside into the cities. City dwellers were forced to burn the woodwork of their homes to keep warm. Everything that could be eaten was eaten, even tulip bulbs. Even so 22,000 people died of hunger and cold. Many more were only saved from death by British airdrops in the weeks leading up to final **liberation** in May 1945.

Food from the sky. British planes drop emergency supplies to the starving Dutch in April 1945.

daily life in the annex so well. He translated sections into German so that his mother could read them. After he had let other people read parts of the diary, a newspaper article appeared praising it. In 1947 a publisher printed a small edition of 1500 copies. It soon sold out, as did a second printing. It was translated into French and German. An English version appeared in 1951. In 1956 the diary became a play, and a movie in 1959. In 1960, 263 Prinsengracht was opened as a museum; 600,000 people visit it each year. Since its first publication, Anne's diary has been translated into 50 languages and over twenty million copies have been sold.

Anne Frank's diary has been published in 50 different languages around the world.

THE DIARY, OR DIARIES?

After Anne decided that her diary might be published one day, she began revising it. The original entries were copied onto single sheets of paper. Some sections were rewritten, some cut out altogether, and some added. The revisions stopped at March 24, 1944.

Miep Gies passed both the original diary and the revised single sheets to Otto Frank. His edition of *Het Achterhuis* (*The Annex*) drew on both versions but also left out passages he thought unimportant, uninteresting, or embarrassing. He also disguised the names of the hiders and helpers, as Anne had, so that their privacy would be protected if the book were ever published.

The diary names are as follows:-

Diary Name	Real Name
Mr. Koophuis	Johannes Kleiman
Mr. Kraler	Victor Kugler
Elli Vossen	Bep Voskuijl
Mr. Vossen	Mr. Voskuijl
Miep van Santen	Miep Gies (originally Miep Santrouschitz)
Henk van Santen	Jan Gies
The van Daan family	The van Pels family
Albert Dussel	Fritz Pfeffer

TRUE OR FALSE?

From the 1950s on, a number of critics began to question whether Anne Frank's diary was genuine. Some insisted that it must be a fake because it was simply too well written to have been produced by a girl of 15. After Otto Frank's death in 1980, he left all Anne's original writings to the government of the Netherlands. They were submitted to careful examination by experts on paper, ink, and handwriting and proved to be completely genuine.

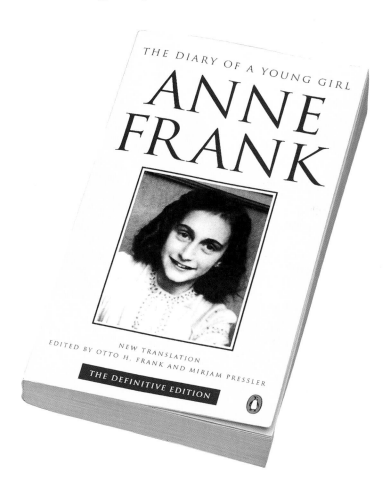

THE DIARY OF A YOUNG GIRL

ANNE FRANK

NEW TRANSLATION
EDITED BY OTTO H. FRANK AND MIRJAM PRESSLER

THE DEFINITIVE EDITION

WHAT PEOPLE THINK ABOUT ANNE FRANK'S DIARY

I hope I shall be able to confide in you completely, as I have never been able to do in anyone before, and I hope that you will be a great support and comfort to me.

Anne Frank, first diary entry,
June 12, 1942

Anne's diary tells a story that is true, memorable, important, and strongly personalized ... compelling reading.
Rabbi Julia Neuberger, 1995

By coincidence I came across a diary that was written during the war. The Netherlands State Institute for War Documentation already has about 200 such diaries, but it would surprise me if there was another one which was as pure, as intelligent, and yet as human as this one.

Professor Jan Romein, historian, 1946

The Diary ... remains astonishing and excruciating ... evidence of her ferocious appetite for life. It gnaws at us still.
The New York Times Book Review,
1995

From time to time she talks about the horrors beyond her window, but most of the diary is about the turmoil within her growing heart. Cooped up, misunderstood, she is every teenager ... she spends her time trying to figure out who will love her as she is and how she will make do with last year's undershirts.

Anna Quindlen, writer, 1994

I'm told that every night when the sun goes down, somewhere in the world the curtain is going up on the stage play made from Anne's diary.... her voice has reached the far edges of the earth.

Miep Gies, helper of the Frank family, 1987

Anne never spoke about hatred anywhere in her diary. She wrote that despite everything, she believed in the goodness of people. And that when the war was over, she wanted to work for the world and for people. This is the duty I have taken over from her. I have received many thousands of letters. Young people especially always want to know how these terrible things could ever have happened. I answer them as well as I can, and I often finish by saying : "I hope that Anne's book will have an effect on the rest of your life so that … you will work for unity and peace."

Otto Frank, father of Anne Frank, 1970

People throughout the world have read Anne's diary and, because it captured so well the feelings and experiences of one of the war's many victims, have made Anne Frank a symbol of the millions of Jews who perished in World War II. Moreover, Anne has become a symbol for all people who are persecuted today for their background, the color of their skin, or their beliefs.

Ruud van der Rol and Rian Verhoeven,
Anne Frank House, 1994

ANNE FRANK: TIMELINE

1889 Otto Frank is born in Frankfurt–am–Main, Germany

1900 Edith Hollander is born in Aachen, Germany

1914 Outbreak of the First World War

1918 (November 11) World War One ends

1919 National Socialist German Workers' Party (**Nazi** party) founded
Versailles Treaty signed

1925 Otto Frank marries Edith Hollander. They settle in Otto's
mother's house in Frankfurt

1926 (November 16) Margot Frank born

1927 The Frank family move to a new home at 307 Marbachweg

1929 Business crisis in United States and Europe causes trade collapse
and mass **unemployment**
(June 12) Anne Frank born

1931 Collapse of German banking system.
The Frank family move to 24 Ganghoferstrasse

1933 (January 30) Hitler becomes Chancellor of Germany
Enabling Law grants Hitler the powers of a **dictator** for four years
Otto Frank moves to Amsterdam. The rest of the family go to
Aachen, Germany.
Edith and Margot join Otto in December.

1934 Anne joins her family in Amsterdam in February and goes to
Montessori school

1935 Anti-Jewish Nuremberg Laws proclaimed

1936 Olympic Games held in Berlin

1938 Germany takes over Austria and the Sudetenland

1939 Germany takes over Bohemia and Moravia and conquers Poland
(September 3) Britain and France declare war on Germany

1940 Otto Frank's business moves to 263 Prinsengracht
(May 10) Germany invades the Netherlands
(May 14) Dutch forces surrender

1941 Otto Frank's Opekta–Works changes its name to Trading
Company Gies & Co.
(September) Margot and Anne Frank transferred to Jewish school
(December 11) Germany invades the Soviet Union and declares
war on the United States

1942 (June 12) Anne receives a diary as a birthday present

(July 6) Frank family go into hiding

(July 13) van Daan (Van Pels) family join the Frank family in the annex

(November 16) Albert Dussel (Fritz Pfeffer) moves into the annex

1943 German army attacking Stalingrad surrenders

Italy surrenders to the Allies

1944 (June 6) Allies invade Normandy

(June 12) Hitler launches V bombing campaign against Britain

(July 20) Hitler survives an attempt to kill him

(August 4) People hiding in the annex are arrested and

(August 8) transported to Westerbork and

(September 3) then to Auschwitz

(September 11) Allied troops reach the borders of Germany

(September) Allied troops free the southern Netherlands

(October) Anne and Margot are transferred to Bergen-Belsen

1945 (January 27) Auschwitz is liberated by the Russian army

(March) Anne and Margot die

(April 30) Hitler kills himself in Berlin

(May 5) **Liberation** of the Netherlands

(May 8) VE (Victory in Europe) Day marks the end of the war in Europe

(June 3) Otto Frank returns to 263 Prinsengracht

1947 Diary published as *The Annex* (*Het Achterhuis*) in Dutch

1951 Diary published in English

1952 Otto Frank moves to Basel, Switzerland

1953 Otto Frank remarries

1956 Anne Frank's Diary is dramatized as a stage play

1957 Anne Frank Foundation established to manage 263 Prinsengracht as a museum

1959 Anne Frank's diary is filmed

1960 263 Prinsengracht opened as a museum

1980 Otto Frank dies

GLOSSARY

Allied forces armed forces of the countries united against an enemy

Aryan member of the highest racial group in the **Nazi** pyramid of human types. The word originally described a group of languages spoken in northern India from which both German and English have developed. Later the word meant people who spoke those languages. They were thought of as ancient race of tough warriors of great beauty and high intelligence.

The language link is a matter of history. The idea of a heroic "master race" has no basis.

brine salt water

calisthenics exercises

communists people who believe in a government based on the idea that a single ruling political party can run a country for all its people's benefit better than if they are left to make their own decisions and keep their own private homes, land and businesses. In practice communist governments have usually been cruel dictatorships.

concentration camp a prison where political opponents could be concentrated together; in theory they were to be "educated" through work and exercise; in practice torture was common

dictator ruler with complete power, not answerable to a governing body

informer person who supplies secret information for money

kale cabbage

liberation setting free

Nazi short name of the National Socialist German Workers' Party (*Nationalsozialistische Deutsche Arbeiterpartei*), led by Adolf Hitler. The Nazis ruled Germany 1933–1945.

neutral not taking sides

pension boarding house

persecution deliberate ill-treatment

ration card, ration coupon documents allowing the holder to buy a limited amount of food or goods

resistance fighting back. The Dutch resistance movement fought against occupation by the Nazis.

SA (*Sturmabteilungen*; Stormtroopers) private army of the Nazi party

swastika (*Hakenkreuz*) official symbol of Nazism; based on an Indian design, associated with the ancient Aryans

synagogue Jewish place of worship

unemployment not having work

More Books to Read

Brown, Gene. *Ann Frank: Child of the Holocaust:* Danbury, CT: Blackbirch Press. 1991.

Epstein, Rachel S. *Anne Frank.* New York: Franklin Watts. 1997.

McDonough, Yona Z. New York: Henry Holt & Company. 1997.

Verhoeven, Rian. *Ann Frank: Beyond the Diary*. New York: Viking Children's Books. 1993.

Index

INVADER ZIM

VOLUME 2

Created by
JHONEN VASQUEZ

VOLUME 2

Writer/Illustrator, Chapter 1 **KC GREEN**

Writer, Chapter 2 **KYLE STARKS**

Writer, Chapter 3, 4 **ERIC TRUEHEART**

Writers, Chapter 5 **DENNIS & JESSIE HOPELESS**

Layouts, Chapter 2-5 **AARON ALEXOVICH**

Illustrator, Chapter 2-5 **DAVE CROSLAND**

Colorist, Chapter 1 **SAVANNA GANUCHEAU**

Letterer, Chapter 1-5 & Colorist, Chapter 2,3,5 **WARREN WUCINICH**

Colorist, Chapter 4 **J. R. GOLDBERG**

Retail cover illustrated by **DAVE CROSLAND** and **WARREN WUCINICH**
Fried Pie variant cover illustrated by **JHONEN VASQUEZ**
Oni Press variant cover by **JHONEN VASQUEZ** and **J.R. GOLDBERG**
Hot Topic variant cover illustrated by **LOUIE DEL CARMEN**

Control Brain **JHONEN VASQUEZ** Designed by **KEITH WOOD**

Edited by **ROBIN HERRERA**

AN ONI PRESS PUBLICATION

Published by Oni Press, Inc.

publisher JOE NOZEMACK
editor in chief JAMES LUCAS JONES
v.p. of marketing & sales ANDREW MCINTIRE
publicity coordinator RACHEL REED
director of design & production TROY LOOK
graphic designer HILARY THOMPSON
digital art technician JARED JONES
managing editor ARI YARWOOD
senior editor CHARLIE CHU
editor ROBIN HERRERA
editorial assistant BESS PALLARES
director of logistics BRAD ROOKS
logistics associate JUNG LEE

This volume collects issues #6-10 of the
Oni Press series *Invader Zim*.

Oni Press, Inc.
1305 SE Martin Luther King Jr. Blvd.
Suite A
Portland, OR 97214
USA

onipress.com · facebook.com/onipress · twitter.com/onipress
onipress.tumblr.com · instagram.com/onipress

First edition: July 2016

ISBN: 978-1-62010-336-4 • eISBN: 978-1-62010-337-1
Fried Pie Exclusive ISBN: 978-1-62010-350-0
Hot Topic Exclusive ISBN: 978-1-62010-358-6
Oni Press Exclusive ISBN: 978-1-62010-348-7

nickelodeon

Library of Congress Control Number: 2015950610

1 3 5 7 9 10 8 6 4 2

PRINTED IN USA.

CHAPTER: 1

illustration by KC GREEN

ZIM'S BAD DAY

...A LOAN.

CERTAINLY SIR, WE CAN TALK LOANS. PLEASE HAVE A SEAT!

A SEEEEAT?

A SEAT IS SOMETHING I HAVE TRAINED FOR FOR WEEKS—

—AND CAN DO MOST RELIABLY!

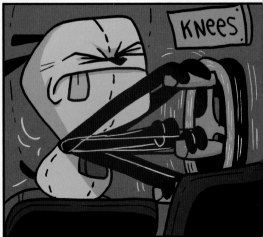

KNEES

SITTING ENGAGED

PFFFFFF

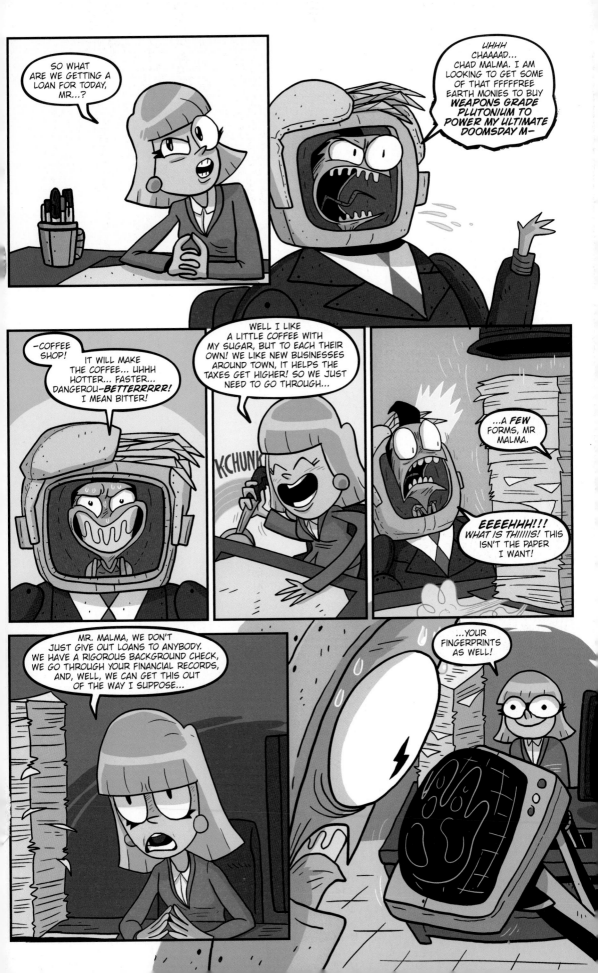

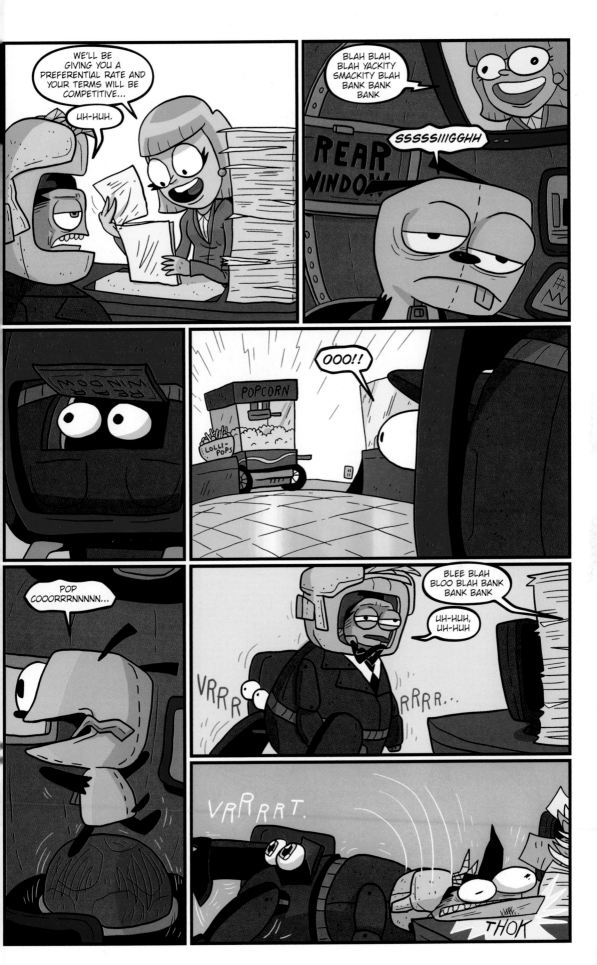

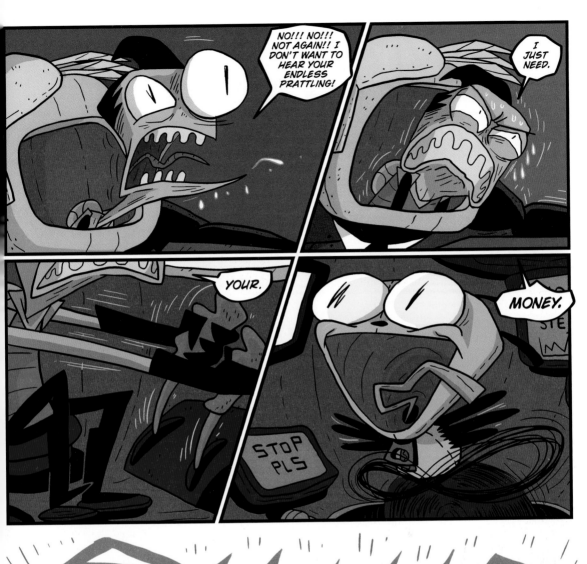

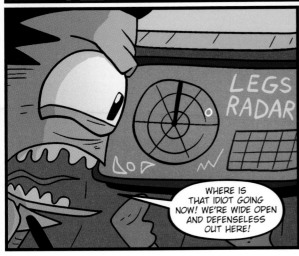

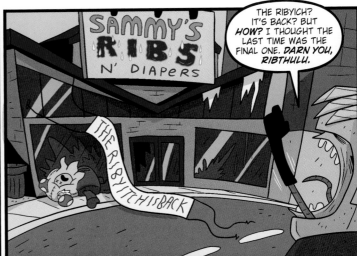

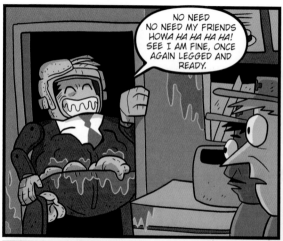

MY BOOT!

SPULNCH

WHAT WAS THAT YOU WERE SAYING, I WAS CHOKING ON YOUR BOOT

I DON'T RECALL! I MUST INSTEAD FIX THE SUITMECH THAT *YOU* BROKE GIR!

BUT I DIDN—

AH AH GIR! IT'S ALREADY SETTLED. I'LL BE DOWN IN THE LAB MAKING THE REPAIRS FOR TOMORROW.

WE'LL GO BACK TO THAT BANK AND GET OUR LOAN JUST YET. KEEP WATCH UP HERE, GIR!

FLUSSSSSSSHHKHH

grgl grgl

MY HEART STOPPED WORKING

good bye.

 CHAPTER: 2

illustration by **DAVE CROSLAND** and **WARREN WUCINICH**

ANOTHER GLORIOUS VICTORY, GIR! WE HAVE SURVIVED BLASTROPOLIS- THE MOST VIOLENT BATTLE-MALL IN ALL OF KNOWN SPACE AND EMERGED WITH A TERRIFYING HAUL OF NEW WEAPON-STUFFS!
SQUIDGYTOMIC LAUNCHERS! GALAXUS ZORM RIFLES! PLETHUVIAN ROCKET FISTS! EVEN A SHLOOGHORGIAN DOOKIE-NIGHTMARE-POD!
EHHEHHE... DOOKIE.
I ONLY NEEDED SPACE-PANTS, BUT WITH THESE, THE EARTH WILL FALL BEFORE ME IN LESS TIME THAN IT TAKES TO JUICE A PLIKUVIAN HOT DOG GOBLIN! THEY'RE FULL OF JUICE, YA KNOW?
ISN'T YOU GONNA ASK ME WHAT I GOT?
EHHH... WELL, WHAT DID YOU G-
I GOT THIS THING!!
AIEEEEGH!
AAAAAAAAAAAAAGHHH!!

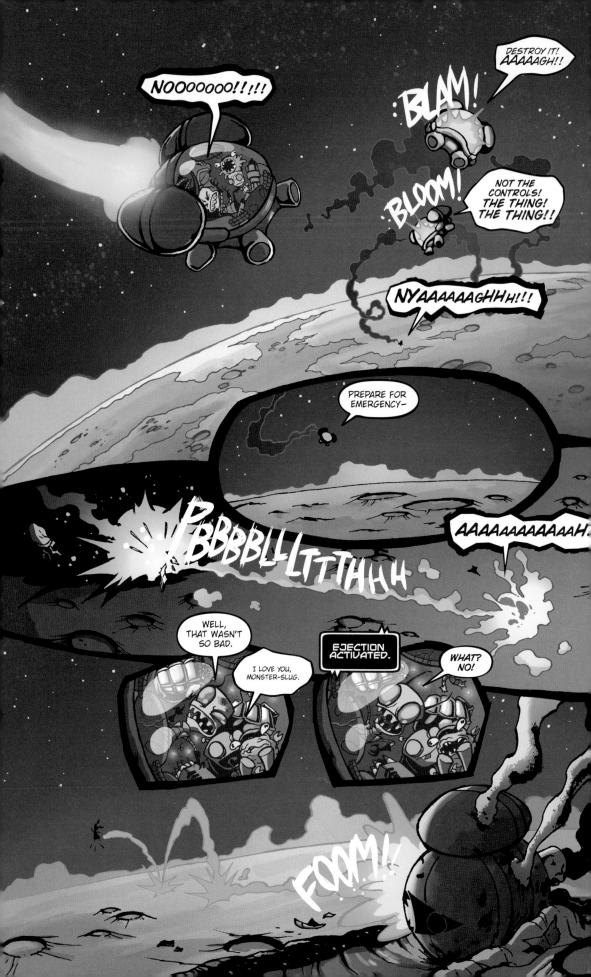

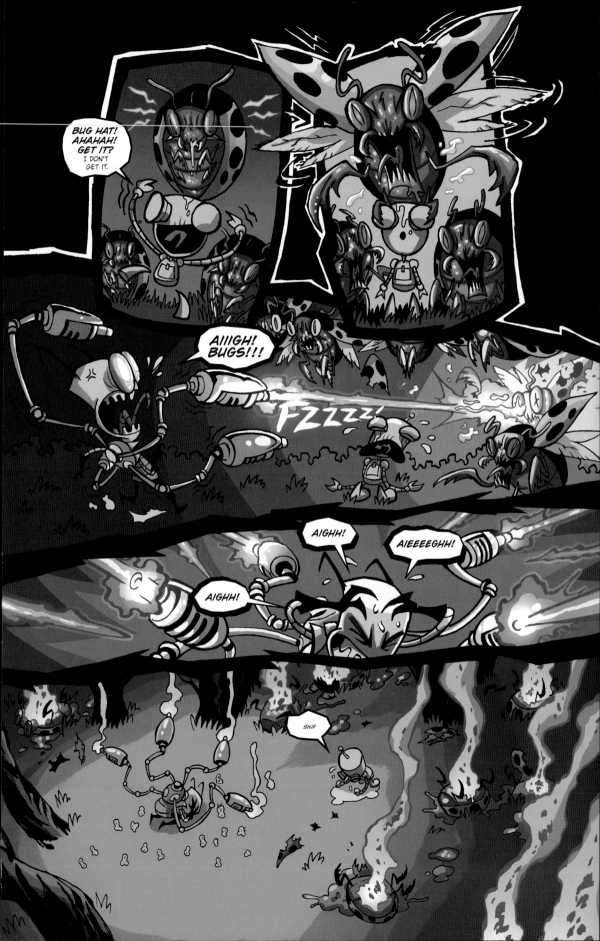

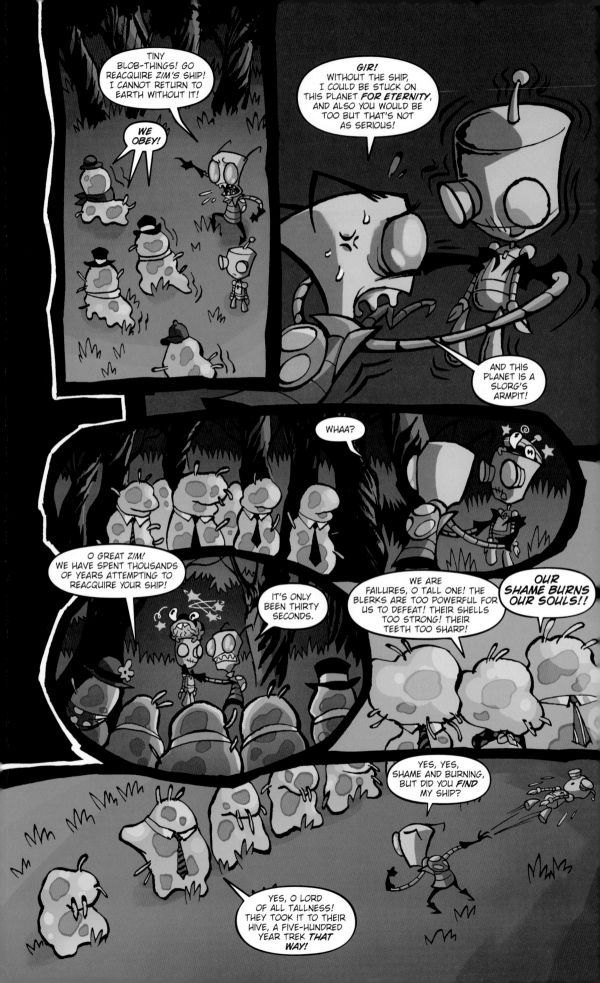

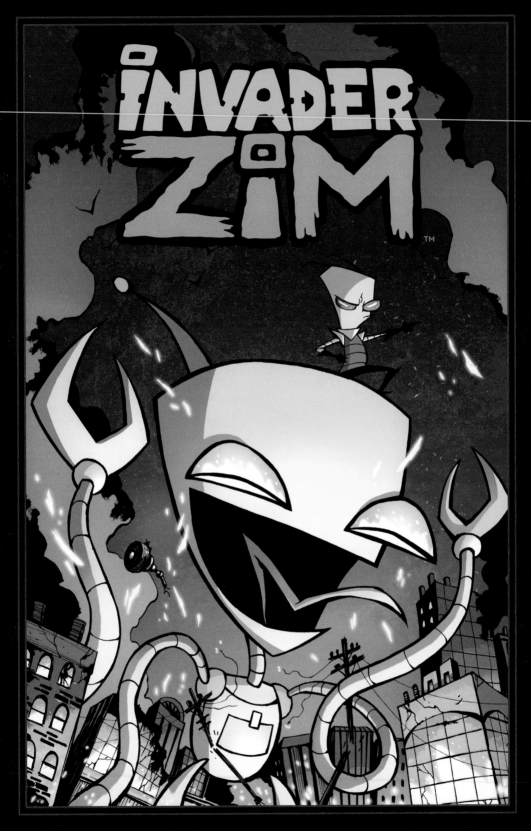

 CHAPTER: 3

illustration by **DAVE CROSLAND** and **WARREN WUCINICH**

IT IS NEARLY TIME, GIR! THIS ALLIANCE WILL SECURE MY PLAN TO DOMINATE THE HUMANS UTTERLY!
UNTIL NOW, I HAVE ONLY DOMINATED THEM SEMI-UTTERLY! BUT TONIGHT ZIM ***EMBRACES THE COMPLETE UTTER!*** NO PARTIALLY UTTER WILL-
GIR! STOP BUILDING A TINY HOBO CAMP ON MY FEET!
MMMMMMMMM! HOBO WEENIE!
SILENCE! THEY HAVE ARRIVED!

SERIOUSLY, WHAT IS *UP* WITH PEOPLE SAYING–!
I MEAN... YES, I'M LEADER OF EARTH.
THEN AS LEADER, IT IS A COURTESY TO SHOW YOU WHO HAS TAKEN OVER YOUR PLANET. OPEN YOUR GIANT HEAD TO MY PSYCHIC VISIONS!
THE NAME OF MY KIND IS INCONCEIVABLE BY YOUR LANGUAGE.
HOW ABOUT "SPACE PANTS?"
OH WAIT, NO, YOU GOT IT. WE ARE *"THE SPACE PANTS!"*
WE EVOLVED ON THE PLANET *SLKSSKZ*, WHERE WE LIVED IN SYMBIOSIS WITH THE LOCAL CREATURES.
BUT WE BURDENED OUR LAND TO EXTINCTION, AND WARS DECIMATED THE PLANET.
NOW WE ARE A SPACE-FARING RACE. LANDING ON PLANETS. SHARING OUR PANTS-SELVES WITH LOCAL CREATURES.
YOU MEAN TAKING THEM OVER!
THEIR LEGS LOOK STUPID.
AND THEN WE RECEIVED A TRANSMISSION FROM THE IRKEN ZIM. HE PROMISED HE WOULD SHARE THIS WORLD WITH US IF WE WORKED WITH HIM.
WAIT- ZIM? *THE* ZIM?!

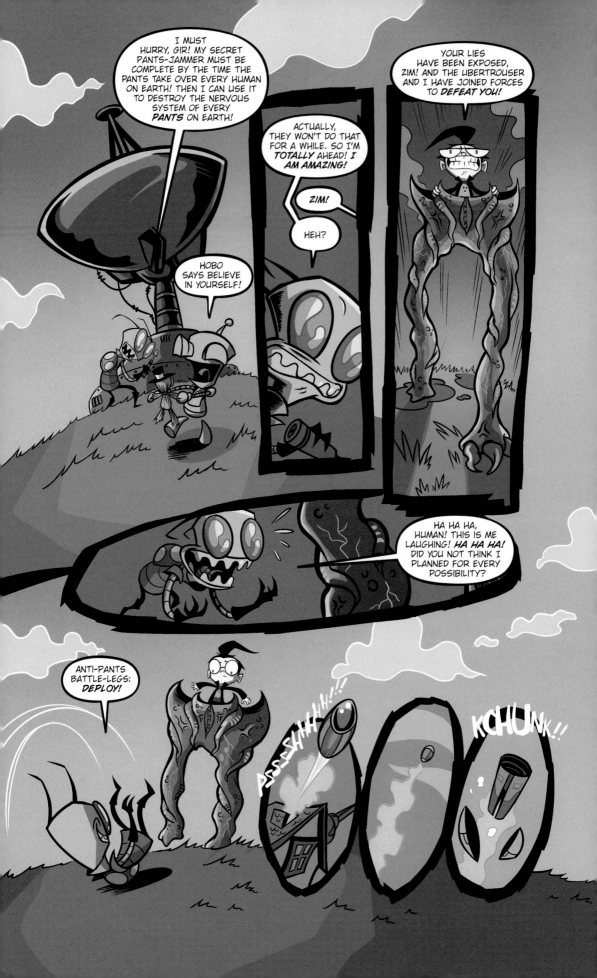

CHAPTER: 4

illustration by DAVE CROSLAND and CASSIE KELLY

AHAHHAHAH! Remember the last issue where the world was invaded by evil space pants? Those pants're gonna haunt my dream-pants forever, which is fine because I LOVED IT, except for the parts that made me so mad. I was hoping they'd get into whether or not space pants wore clothes, but I GUESS the writers don't care about real issues! UGH! HEH! This issue looks good, though. I flipped through it and Dib's real weird looking in it. like Weirder than usual. Hopefully the writers explain why everyone says Dib's head is big when, really, everyone has big heads! I'm gonna get a soda.

Recap Kid by WARREN WUCINICH

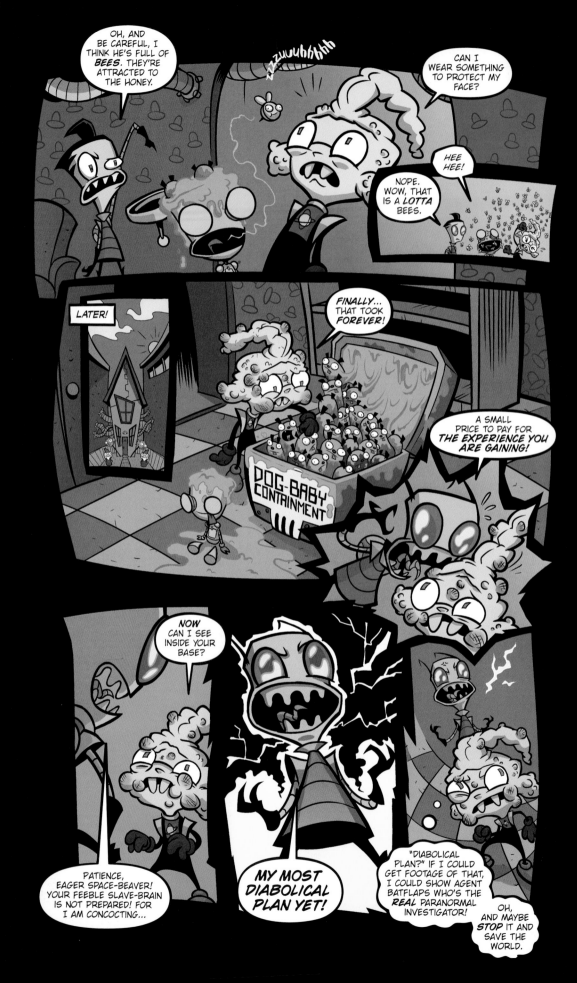

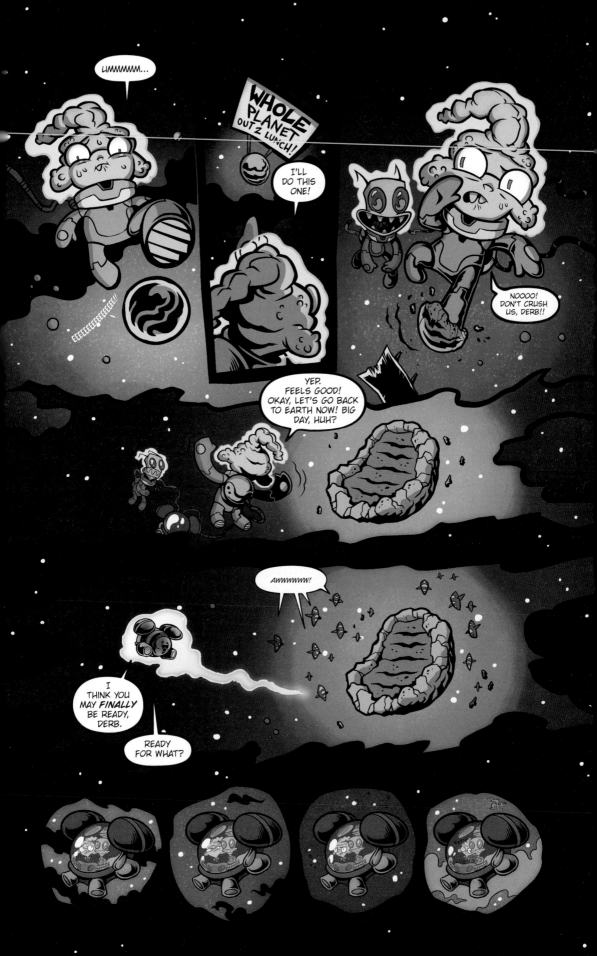

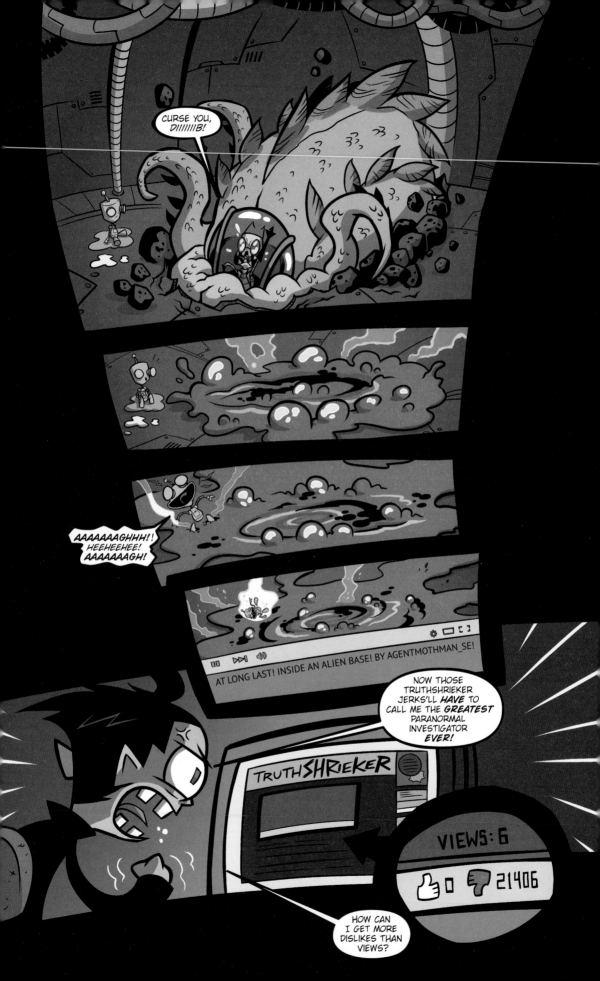

COMMENTS

 HOBOTRONIC16
Fake.

 CPT.MONKEYBUTTONS
Obviously Photoshmooped, and BADLY at that. I can still see the strings!

 ZIMFAN4000
Guys of COURSE it's fake, but it's my favorite show! The guy who plays Mothman is AWESOME and I LIKE that he's ugly! I hope they get a new puppet to play ZIM. 5 Stars.

 HUNKoFSADNESS
How can aliens be real if I'm not real?

 CONSPIRACY_JOSH
Frist!

 **CORNFLUKES**
This video wastes my life. I want a refund.

 **UNICORN_PIE**
I can't reference a meme that properly covers my hatred of this video.

 RUMPLESHEAD
Is this the same Mothman who's dating my mom? Stop it! Nobody likes you! Stop it!

 **AGENT_BATFLAPS**
Mothman STINKS! Check out MY video: HELP, I'M STUCK IN AN ALIEN BASE, AND HERE'S TWO HOURS OF MY FEET TO PROVE IT.

 **FLAPS4EVA**
AWESOME COMMENT, BATFLAPS! I haven't watched your video but it's the best video EVER! I LOVE YOU!

HEY, DIB! I CAN HEAR YOU CRYING THROUGH THE WALL! SHUTUP!

 END.

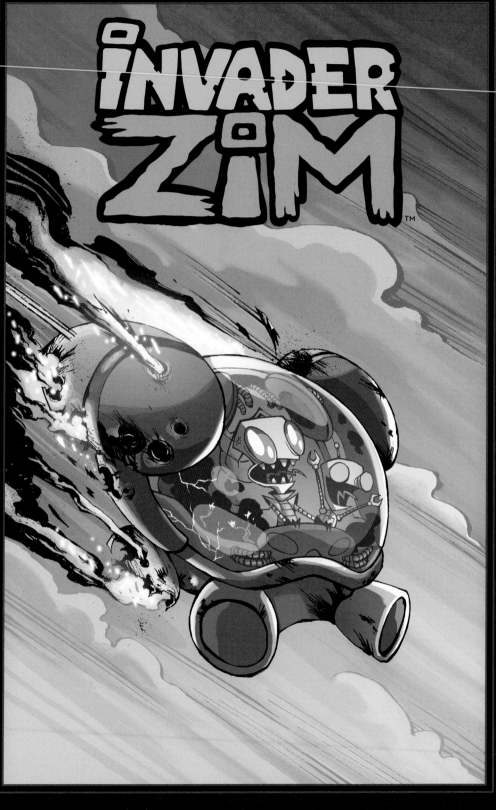

CHAPTER: 5

illustration by **DAVE CROSLAND** and **WARREN WUCINICH**

Recap Kid by **WARREN WUCINICH**

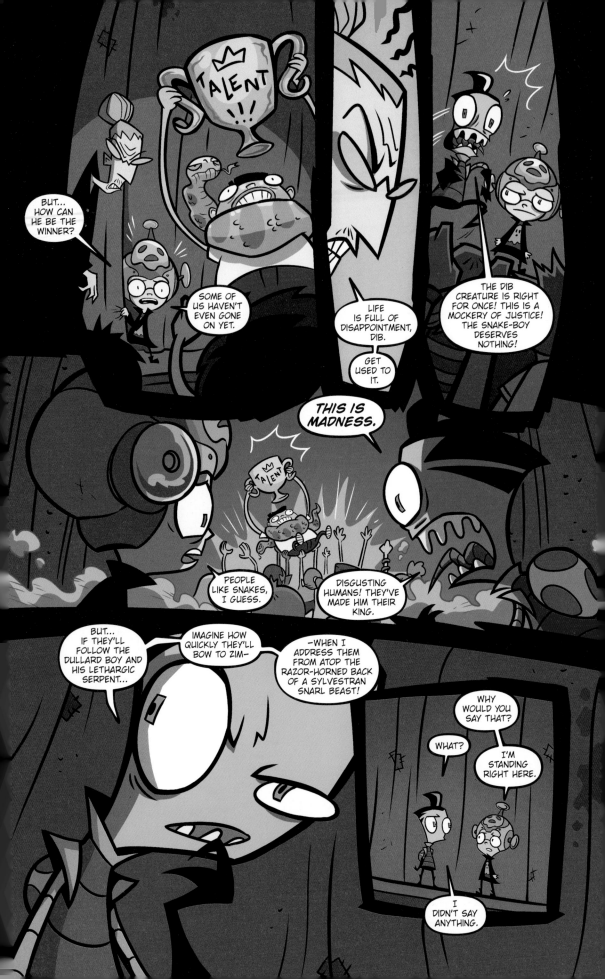

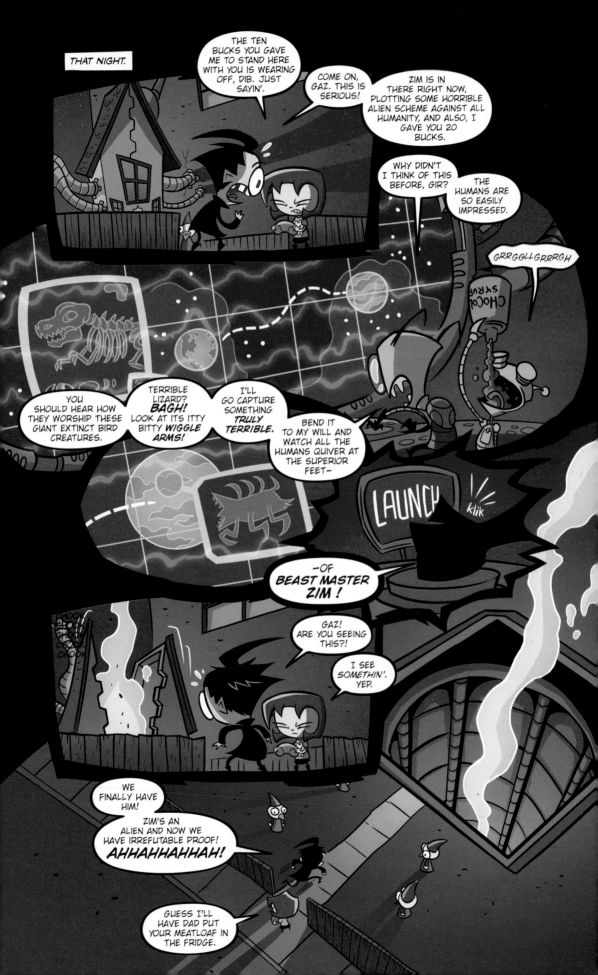

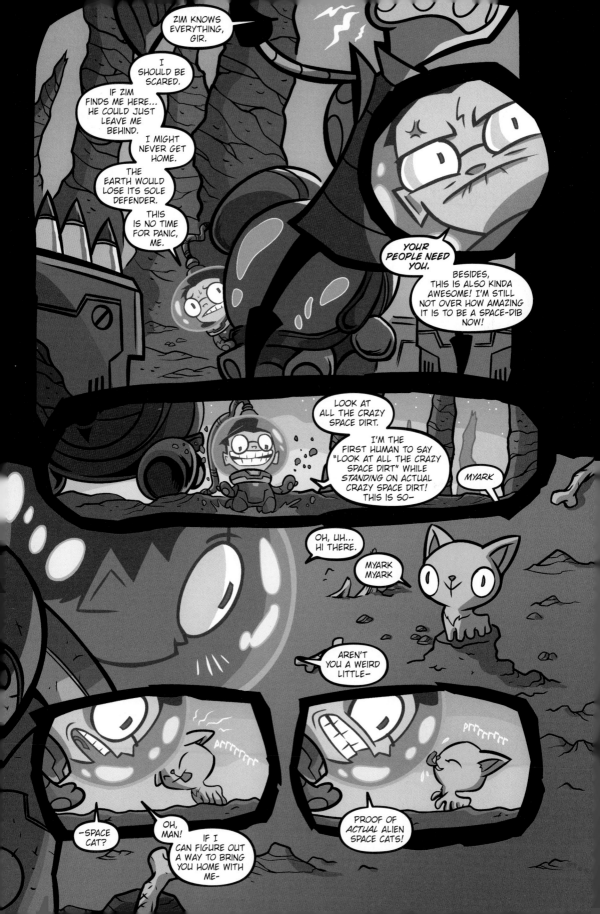

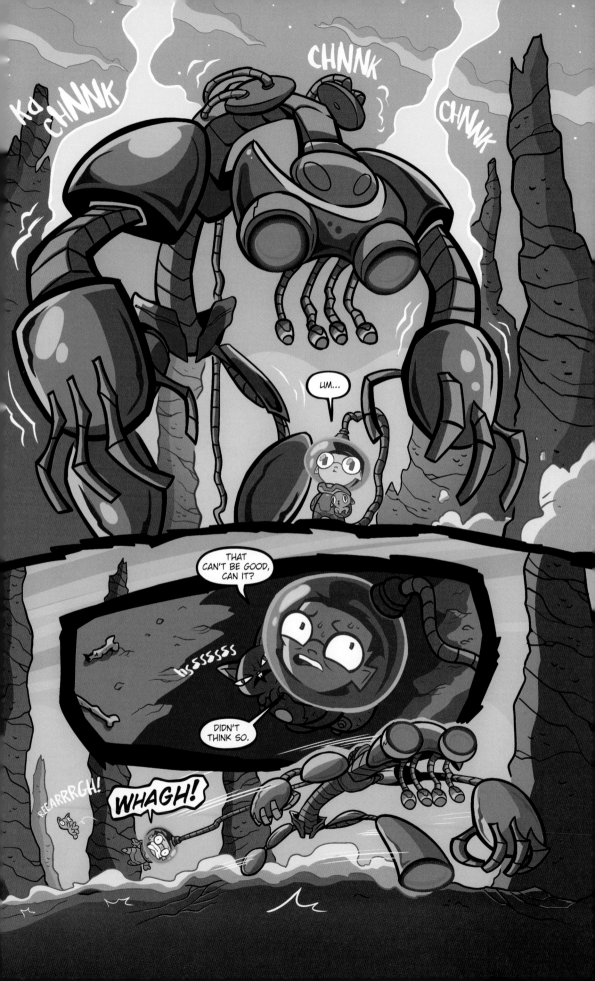

"INVADER WHO?"

BONUS SHORT BY
KC GREEN

INVADER ZIM ™

"ACTIVITY TIME"

BONUS SHORT BY
EDMUND MCMILLEN

IT'S ACTIVITY TIME!

BY EDMUND

SPOT THE DIFFERENCE!

CAN YOU SPOT ALL 8? WELL CAN YOU!? HEY! I'M TALKING TO YOU!

CAN YOU FIND A FISH, A CAN, A HIGH HEEL, A CHEESE A PACMAN, A KNIFE, A WHALE, A PIZZA AN EVIL PENGUIN, AN EARTH WORM, A FIBBLE, A ZILBER AND A TUNK?

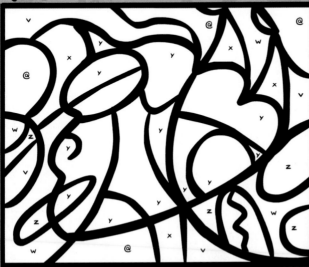

COLOR BY NUMBER!

V=BLACK W=MAROON X=PINK Y=BROWN Z=PURPLE @=GOLD

DRESS UP ZIM!

MINI FLIP!

IT IS SUCH A FRIGHTFUL SIGHT! I MEAN HONESTLY HOW WAS
ONE TO HAVE AN EXPLANATION FOR THIS? IS DIB ACTUALLY
A DRIPPY, BLOATED, PIG KNUCKLED BUBBA FULL OF SOUR CREAM!?

LICK THAT PIGGY!

HELP GIR LICK THAT PIG BUT AVOID THOSE IMPOSTER TONGUES!

MATCH the FOOT!

DRAW A LINE FROM THE HEAD TO ITS
MATCHING FOOT! AND REMEMBER TO
REALLY DIG INTO THAT PAGE, KIDS!

I DUMB

ANSWER: 23, B, 12, $, CORN, 81

CREATORS

JHONEN VASQUEZ

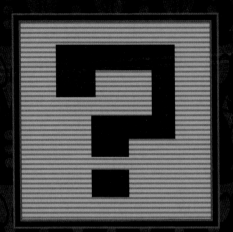

Jhonen Vasquez is a writer and artist who walks in many worlds, not unlike Blade, only without having to drink blood-serum to survive the curse that is also his greatest power (still talking about Blade here). He's worked in comics and animation and is the creator of *Invader ZIM*, a fact that haunts him to this day.

@JhonenV

ERIC TRUEHEART

ERIC CAN'T DRAW

Eric Trueheart was one of the original writers on the *Invader ZIM* television series back when there was a thing called "television." Since then, he's made a living writing moderately-inappropriate things for people who make entertainment for children, including Dreamworks Animation, Cartoon Network, Disney TV, PBS, Hasbro and others. Upon reading this list, he now thinks he maybe should have become a dentist, and he hates teeth.

@erictrueheart

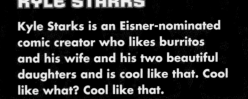

KYLE STARKS

Kyle Starks is an Eisner-nominated comic creator who likes burritos and his wife and his two beautiful daughters and is cool like that. Cool like what? Cool like that.

@TheKyleStarks

@HopelessDent

@jessie_hopeless

DENNIS HOPELESS

Dennis Hopeless is the Harvey Award winning and New York Times best-selling writer of *Avengers Arena*, *X-Men* and *Spider-Woman*. He has the heart of a man twice his age.

JESSIE HOPELESS

Jessie Hopeless is an accomplished tattoo artist, mediocre piano player and her favorite cupcake is cherry chip. She has story-edited and co-plotted dozens of comics over the years but *Invader ZIM* is her first writing credit.

The Hopelesses live in Kansas City

@essrose

AARON ALEXOVICH

Aaron Alexovich's first professional art job was drawing deformed children for Nickelodeon's *Invader ZIM*. Since then he's been deforming children for various animation and comic projects, including *Avatar: The Last Airbender, Randy Cunningham: 9th Grade Ninja, Disney's Haunted Mansion, Fables, Kimmie66, ELDRITCH!* (with art by Drew Rausch) and three volumes of his own beloved horror/comedy witch comic dealie, *Serenity Rose*.

@DaveCrosland

DAVE CROSLAND

was born in Buffalo, NY and fought his way through the baneful hordes to adulthood in Los Angeles, CA. He's created art for comics, cartoons, concert posters, video games and more. Along with *Invader ZIM*, his memorable projects include *Randy Cunningham: 9th Grade Ninja, Scarface: Scarred for Life, Everybody's DEAD, Yo Gabba Gabba* and his autobio comic *EGO REHAB*. When he isn't drinking rum from the skulls of his foes, Dave can be found hoarding pets and eating all your peanut butter.

KC GREEN

@kcgreenn

lives like he breathes: Often. He was 13 when Invader Zim came on tv, so look at me now, DAD. He made *Graveyard Quest* that came out from Oni, too. And he draws comics online! Is a link okay? You can go here kcgreenndotcom.com, thank you!

WARREN WUCINICH

@warrenwucinich

Warren Wucinich an illustrator, colorist and part-time carny currently living in Durham, NC. When not making comics he can usually be found watching old *Twilight Zone* episodes and eating large amounts of pie.

SAVANNA GANUCHEAU

is a comic artist from New Orleans, Louisiana currently living in Melbourne, Victoria. Previously, she's drawn shorts in *Lumberjanes: Makin' The Ghost Of It* and *Boom Studios' BOOM! Box 2015 Mix Tape #1*. She's also done coloring work for *Toe Tag Riot*, *The Ruby Equation*, and *Invader Zim*. She's a friendly young lady who loves all things cute. She's usually on twitter wasting time. So, please feel free to tweet at her: @srganuch!

@ Srganuch

J.R. GOLDBERG

J.R. is a visual designer and illustrator who has worked in comics and animation. Not only is she responsible for making sure your eyes love the colors on the *Invader ZIM* pages, but she is responsible for all color in reality. If you see in color, thank J.R. for allowing this. Thank you, J.R. Goldberg. Thank you. She currently works and lives inside the color turquoise.

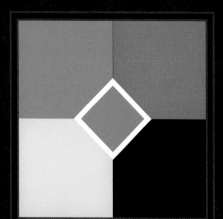

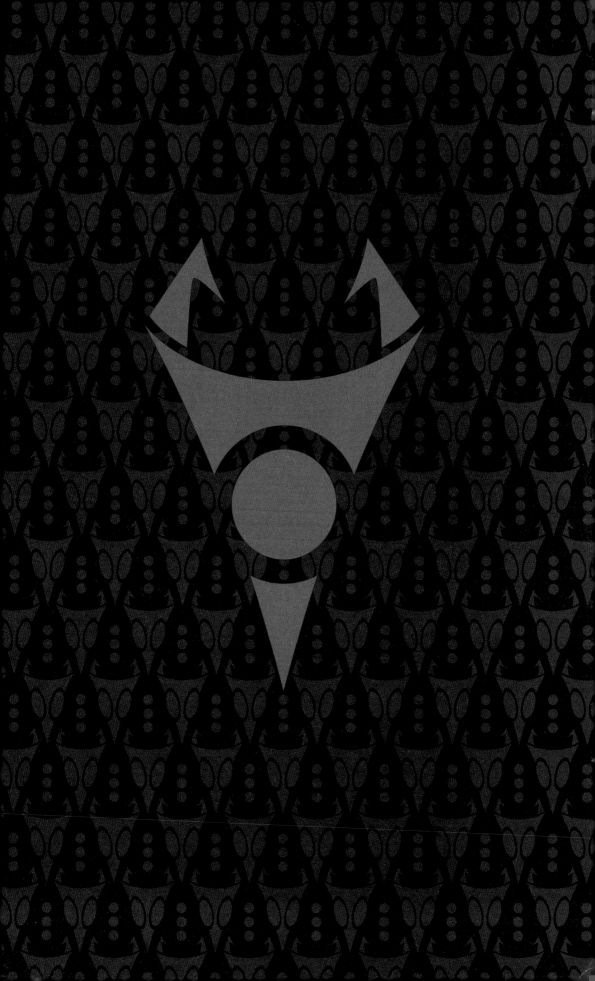

MORE BOOKS FROM ONI PRESS...